THE PEACE, LOVE &
POTATO SALAD
COOKBOOK

COOKBOOK **24** DELICIOUS RECIPES

The Story of a Crowd-Sourced $55,492 Bowl of Potato Salad

THE PEACE, LOVE & POTATO SALAD COOKBOOK

24 DELICIOUS RECIPES

ZACK BROWN
AND TERESA BLACKBURN

SPRING HOUSE PRESS

Publishers: Paul McGahren and Matthew Teague
Design: J Spinks
Photography: Danielle Atkins
Food Styling and Recipe Development: Teresa Blackburn
Copy Editor: Joel Showalter

Spring House Press
3613 Brush Hill Court
Nashville, TN 37216
ISBN 13: 978-1-940611-38-9
Library of Congress Control Number: 2016935448
Printed in China
First Printing: July 2016

Note: The following list contains names used in *The Peace, Love, & Potato Salad Cookbook*
that may be registered with the United States Copyright Office: Kickstarter, Facebook, Google, Google
Hangout, Columbus Dispatch, Oculus Rift, *Veronica Mars*, *Reading Rainbow*, *The New York Times*,
Wall Street Journal, *USA Today*, *The New Yorker*, *The A.V. Club*, *Good Morning America*, Homage,
Twitter, Reddit, ABC Studios, ESPN, NFL, WWCD, Columbus Foundation

To learn more about Spring House Press books, or to find a retailer near you,
email info@springhousepress.com or visit us at www.springhousepress.com.

CONTENTS

FOREWORD

Potato Salad never used to be a thing. I mean, it's always been a thing, but until some guy raised $55,492 for a bowl of potato salad on Kickstarter, it was never a thing. It's always just been potato salad. A compound common noun. And then, for a second, it was Potato Salad. When you would write or say "Potato Salad," you'd have to capitalize it. Like people's names and places and God.

I'm not saying Potato Salad was God. But something about potato salad's ascension to Potato Salad—from unremarkable to remarkable—strikes me as noteworthy. I think it's how all of us, whether we were backers or co-conspirators, or culture reporters working on deadline, or Internet trolls, imbued a common thing with greater meaning. Anybody who contributed money, or yelled "Hey, Potato Salad Guy!" at Zack, or asked "What's this Potato Salad thing that Facebook won't shut up about?"—it felt like we were all in on the joke together. It was really nice being in on the joke together. And together, we turned lowly potato salad into something more.

We like to capitalize the things we revere. It's like that tree in the woods where you'd meet all your friends to do kid stuff. It was the Tree. All summer long, the Tree was the gathering point. It's where we all went to connect with one another. And then at the end of the summer, it went back to being a tree.

Potato Salad was the Tree for my friends and me during the summer of 2014. That's where we met you. Potato Salad was how we all connected that summer, how we're connecting now as you read this. And though it's no longer a thing, it still connects us. We can all look back and fondly remember that time when we were all laughing together. It may not be a thing, but it's still special.

Thank you for laughing with us. Thank you for making Potato Salad special.

Mike Stempler
Co-Conspirator

INTRODUCTION

Hey there. I'm Zack Brown, the creator of the Potato Salad Kickstarter. And what you're holding in your hands is, in my opinion, the best potato salad cookbook in the history of the world. This is no exaggeration.

Over the past year, I've discovered that potato salad is more than just a side dish. As you'll see inside this book, it's a true jack-of-all-trades.

It's a classic herald of long summer days and the last hurrah before battening down for a brisk fall and a cold winter. Like the word "aloha," potato salad can be used in both greeting and parting from summer.

Warm potato salads are the perfect way to say *guten tag* to autumn and Oktoberfest. And nothing pairs better with lederhosen and a boot full of dark German beer than a belly full of potatoes and vinegar. Mmmm-mm.

For Thanksgiving and Christmas dinner, sweet potato salads are a great addition to the table. They're the perfect way to celebrate family, gifts, and those few moments when we weren't being absolutely horrible to our country's indigenous people.

And a Caesar potato salad tossed with olives, artichokes, and feta will have you ready to shed your winter clothes and do whatever it is we do in spring. Vote? Do we vote in spring?

Apparently—and I didn't know this until recently—the only requirements for a dish to be called "potato salad" is that it have (1) potatoes of some kind and (2) at least one other ingredient. Isn't that crazy?! So, like, mashed potatoes and gravy? According to some people, that's a kind of potato salad!

So potato salad may be as limitless as the universe itself, contained solely by the boundaries of the human imagination.

As I said, this is the best potato salad cookbook in the history of the world. That's because it was put together by one of the most talented groups of people I have ever had the privilege of working with.

The recipes in this book are so amazing because Teresa Blackburn worked really hard to make them delicious. Teresa has worked as a food stylist for commercial, editorial, film, television, and video for over 25 years, and she blogs at foodonfifth.com.

The photos in this book are so beautiful because Danielle Atkins is a kick-ass food photographer. (Am I allowed to say "kick-ass" in a cookbook?) Danielle shot all the images over three days in Teresa's beautiful home, under the creative direction of J Spinks. My job was simple: I was the taster. In three days, I ate nearly two gallons of potato salad. They were creamy and crunchy, some of them warm, some of them cold, each of them better than the last . . . . Anyway, Danielle takes photos of nearly everything and can be found at DanielleAtkins.com.

The words in this book sound rill good because of copy editor Joel Showalter.

The cover of this book is so sweet in part because of Oliver Brotzge's concept illustrations.

Finally, every detail of the book is so aesthetically pleasing because J Spinks made it so. J brought this concept to Teresa and Danielle, reached out to Joel and Oliver for help, and laid out the whole thing to near perfection. This book was a team effort, and J was our coach through the whole process.

So thank you for buying this book! If you were one of our Kickstarter backers, thank you for backing Potato Salad. If you're just borrowing a friend's book or reading this at a bookstore, stop reading and go buy the book already! What are you doing reading the introduction, anyway? The recipes in this book are amazing. Go make some potato salad right now!

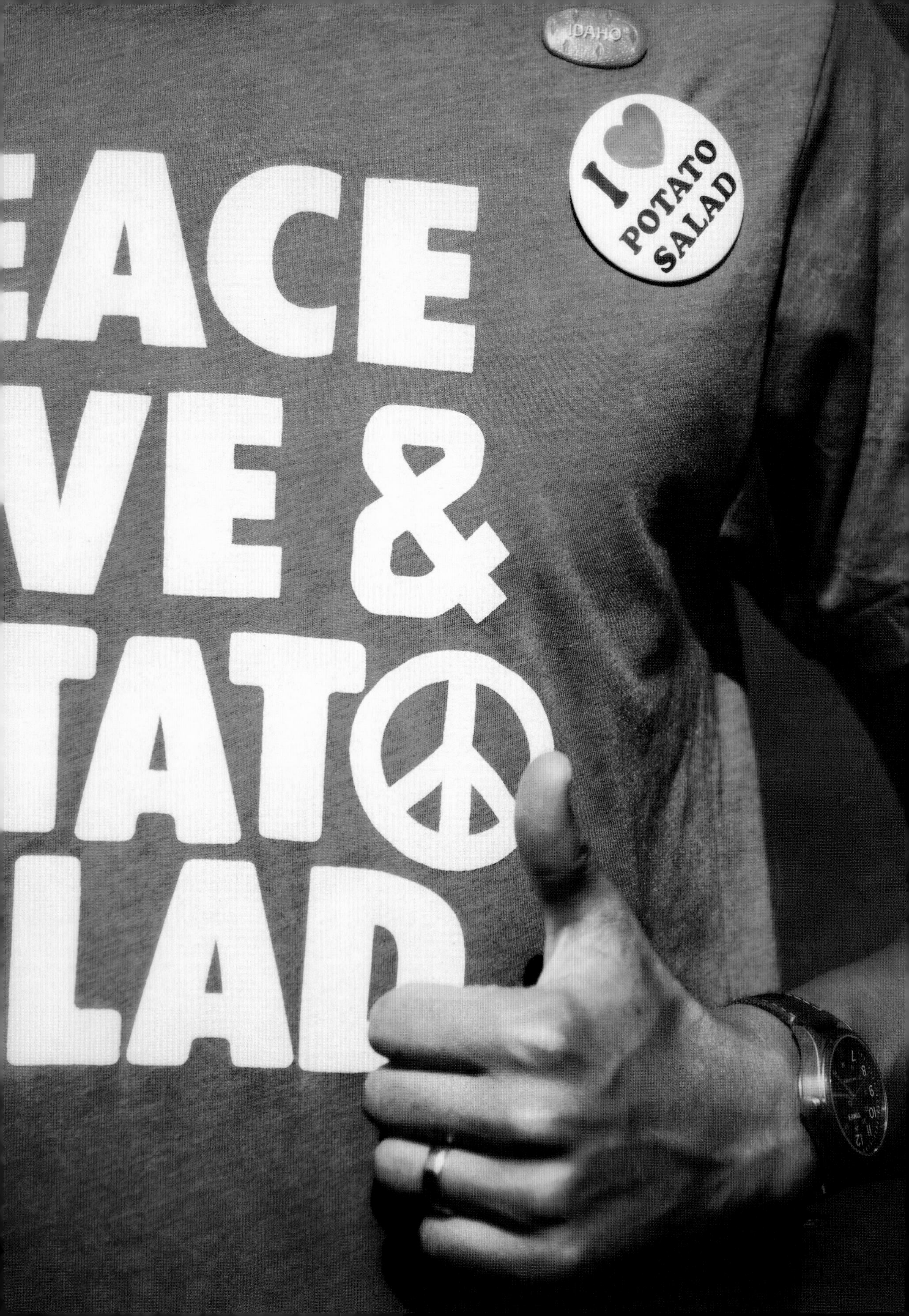
IDAHO
I POTATO SALAD
EACE
VE &
TAT
LAD

A $55,492 BOWL OF POTATO SALAD

This all started on Google Hangout. I keep a persistent chat open with a few of my closest friends. We are in near-constant communication—so much that we periodically start a new hangout so searching the archive of text, photos, and gifs won't be such a pain.

Frances posted an article from the *Columbus Dispatch,* our local newspaper, with the headline "Tradition demands potato salad from aunt." We thought the article was pretty funny. Not in a mean way. But, it was a serious article—in the newspaper—about potato salad! Every time I read the words "potato salad," I had a good chuckle.

We started talking about how much we were looking forward to the Fourth of July. The article had Erica hankering for potato salad. She suggested that we throw a potato salad party. She and her husband David had recently started renting a new place with a huge bathroom. We joked that we could make a whole bathtub-ful of potato salad and have a cocktail party in there.

A few minutes later, I wrote, "I want to launch a really small Kickstarter for this potato salad." Casey chimed in, "For $1 you get a 'thank you' and put on the potato salad mailing list (and a sniff)."

An hour later, I completed a draft of the Potato Salad Kickstarter. The title I chose was "Potato Salad" and the description was "Basically I'm just making potato salad. I haven't decided what kind yet." Backers who pledged three dollars or more were promised a bite of the potato salad. A limited number of supporters would be offered potato-themed haikus. And I promised every backer that I would say their name out loud while making the potato salad.

At this point, I assumed Kickstarter was going to step in and put an end to the whole thing. This kind of campaign would never be approved. Kickstarter was, in my mind, a place for serious projects. Big projects. Oculus Rift, *Veronica Mars, Reading Rainbow,* whatever Zack Braff's working on these days. These are the kinds of things I was used to seeing on the site.

And then, they approved it. We were live.

In the first minute of the campaign, Casey put us over the funding goal with a pledge of 20 dollars. We doubled our goal in less than a minute! (How many Kickstarter campaigns can say that?) In two hours, we were at 10 times our goal. One hundred dollars for a bowl of potato salad.

Three hours after going live, I got a call from a reporter covering the story. That afternoon, the Potato Salad Kickstarter received the first of its 2,068 media mentions. Over the next few days, our weird little Kickstarter project would be written about in every conceivable news publication. *The New York Times, Wall Street Journal, USA Today, The New Yorker,* and many other publications people only read in airports—they all wrote about our potato salad project. The A.V. Club called me "the harbinger of the Fall of the Ironic Empire." (That one actually hurt a little.) The point is, things took off quickly.

By the end of the first day, 44 backers had pledged $176. I remember a friend saying, "What happens if you actually raise $500 to make potato salad?" None of us could have predicted just how crazy this was going to get.

———————————————

The second day of the campaign was the Fourth of July. The potato salad Super Bowl. The holiday must be for potato salad manufacturers what Tax Day is for CPAs.

That evening, I went to see fireworks with some friends. We couldn't keep our eyes off our phones. The local news stations were talking about the Kickstarter. The total kept climbing, much more rapidly than before. Near the end of the night, as "I'm Proud to Be an American" was playing, the total surpassed $1,000.

We were dumbstruck. How was this even possible? What had happened? If you'd told me at the beginning of the week that I was going to make $1,000 "for potato salad," not only would I not have believed you, I wouldn't even have understood what you were trying to tell me. This was the moment, sitting on the bleachers at a local high school, watching a neighborhood fireworks display, when we decided that this money was an opportunity to give back.

But it didn't stop there.

By the end of the weekend, 1,014 people had given me $6,296 to make potato salad. A local vintage clothing brand, Homage, had committed to making a potato salad themed T-shirt. And I had been scheduled to appear on *Good Morning America*. It was overwhelming. Sleep was impossible.

I sat on the couch all Sunday night, wide awake, scrolling Twitter mentions and checking the total as it kept climbing. People all over the world were taking about it. Every couple of seconds, there was a new tweet. I became addicted to Googling "potato salad kickstarter." I hopped from Twitter to Google to Reddit and back again.

Tuesday was a very weird day. I woke up in New York City, having flown in late the night before. The day started at 5 a.m. with a call from a Canadian radio program. An hour later, I walked into ABC Studios in Times Square.

And then I was on live television, talking to the anchors of *Good Morning America.* It was a moment in my life where I felt completely untethered from reality. If I had taken a second to consider how unqualified I was to be speaking to these people, I would have been petrified. George Stephanopoulos was the White House press secretary when I was in high school. Robin Roberts was on ESPN when I was seven. And Michael Strahan was an indisputable NFL great.

During the broadcast, the anchors asked me how I was planning on spending my windfall. I couldn't help but infer that they felt my gains were ill gotten, that I had somehow mulcted my backers out of their cash. I explained that we had all decided to give the money to a charity. I said that we were going to throw a "benefit concert" and that the whole internet would be invited. (That last part was an on-the-spot improvisation.)

The rest of my day in New York was spent shuttling from television studio to television studio, answering the same handful of questions. I repeated the "benefit concert" idea a few more times before the end of the day. There was no backing out now.

By the end of Tuesday, the Potato Salad Kickstarter had 5,289 backers pledging a total of $43,162.

We got to work planning the concert as soon as I got back to Ohio. The idea was a full day of peace, love, and potato salad. In six weeks, we lined up eight local bands, a huge venue on a green space in downtown Columbus, a local radio sponsor in WWCD, and a locally owned restaurant daft enough to commit to help me make 450 pounds of potato salad. (Major props, Piada!) And somewhere during the process, the Kickstarter ended, with a final tally of $55,492 and 6,911 supporters. Insane.

We dubbed the event PotatoStock, and on a Saturday in late September, roughly 2,500 people showed up. Attendees drove in from Cleveland, Montreal, and Washington, D.C. One guy even flew in from the UK. All of the potato salad was eaten, and the event raised $15,000 through corporate sponsorship.

The money was used to start a fund at the Columbus Foundation, a nonprofit philanthropic advisor. Our fund's mission is to support organizations working to end hunger and homelessness in central Ohio. In fact, a portion of the proceeds from the book you're holding will go to support this cause. And best of all, these types of funds accumulate interest and grow over time, so while our little Internet joke will one day be forgotten, its impact will be felt forever.

A NOTE FROM TERESA

Little did I know when I sat down with J Spinks at a local coffee shop last year to discuss "something he thought I might be interested in" that I would soon be immersed in Zack Brown's world of potato salad.

J and I hit it off the first time we met on a photo shoot, and I am so pleased that he thought of me for this project. The words that came out of my mouth were "yes" and "how many recipes do you need and when?" I was smitten with the entire endeavor from the start. I immediately Googled Zack Brown and the Potato Salad Kickstarter and was amazed at what he had orchestrated and accomplished, all via random musings on this humble staple of every summer picnic.

A virtual vortex of recipe ideas, emails and introductions led to a wonderful collaboration among J, Zack, photographer Danielle Atkins, and me. "Peace, Love and Potato Salad" grew and came alive from all our work in my little kitchen, amid pots of boiling potatoes and pans of roasting potatoes, all being tossed and drizzled and tasted. It was really playing while working, with bits of zany hilarity thrown in, while Danielle's camera clicked away. A true labor of love via potato salad.

I hope you enjoy these recipes as much as we did.

Peace and love,
Teresa Blackburn

RECIPES

SUMMER

FALL

WINTER

BLUE CHEESE BABY BEET POTATO SALAD	53
SWEET POTATO SALAD WITH FRESH GINGER & ORANGE	54
GERMAN BAKED POTATO SALAD	57
WINTER SQUASH POTATO SALAD WITH SAGE-FETA DRESSING	58
BLACK-EYED PEA POTATO SALAD	61
CARAMELIZED ONION BREAKFAST POTATO SALAD WITH BACON, EGGS & SPICY PEPPER TOPPING	62

SPRING

GREEN BEAN & FINGERLING POTATO SALAD	66
SMASHED RED POTATO SALAD	69
OLIVE, ARTICHOKE & FETA NEW POTATO SALAD	70
EGG, APPLE & TROUT POTATO SALAD WITH CIDER DRESSING	73
PANZANELLA POTATO SALAD	74
SALT-COOKED FINGERLING POTATO SALAD & GARLIC-CILANTRO MOJO	77

SUMMER

THE CLASSIC POTATO SALAD

This basic recipe (without the balsamic vinegar and radishes) is pretty much the version many of us grew up with. Pickles, pickle juice, and cooked eggs were present in most of those recipes. Since then, potato salad has grown up and stepped into the modern, international world of cuisine—but there's still nothing like a classic.

SERVES 8

2 pounds red-skinned potatoes, peeled and cut into 1-inch chunks

1 cup mayonnaise

2 tablespoons white balsamic vinegar

2 teaspoons salt

1 teaspoon sugar

½ teaspoon ground black pepper

¼ cup diced red onion

¼ cup chopped dill pickles

¼ cup pickle juice

2 hard-cooked eggs, chopped

½ cup thinly sliced radishes

Salt and black pepper to taste

DIRECTIONS

1. Cover potatoes with cold, salted water and bring to a boil. Reduce heat and simmer until tender. Drain and cool.

2. In a large bowl, stir together the mayonnaise, vinegar, salt, sugar, and pepper until well mixed.

3. Add potatoes, onion, pickles, pickle juice, and eggs, gently tossing together. Sprinkle radishes over mixture, then cover and chill. Right before serving, taste, and adjust seasonings, adding salt and black pepper if desired.

 TIP Red-skinned potatoes are round or oblong and have a bright white flesh. They're waxy and moist, with a creamy texture and wonderful earthy flavor. These potatoes are excellent for recipes such as this one because they hold their shape when cooked.

LEMONY POTATO SALAD WITH MICROGREENS

This easy-to-prepare potato salad has a light flavor, thanks to the delicate microgreens and a generous portion of fresh lemon juice. You can serve this potato salad at room temperature or chilled, and it goes great with grilled fish or chicken.

SERVES 6

2 pounds Yukon gold potatoes, peeled and cut into chunks

2 small shallots, minced

1 teaspoon red wine vinegar

2 teaspoons stone-ground mustard

1 generous teaspoon grated lemon zest

2 teaspoons fresh lemon juice

Salt and black pepper to taste

2 tablespoons olive oil

2 cups of microgreens

DIRECTIONS

1. Put potatoes in a saucepan and cover with cold water. Bring to a boil, then turn heat down and simmer potatoes until tender. Drain.

2. For dressing, stir together shallots, vinegar, mustard, lemon zest, lemon juice, salt, and pepper. Whisk in olive oil until well combined.

3. Place warm potatoes in a bowl, drizzle with dressing and toss gently. Cool to room temperature.

4. When ready to serve, add microgreens, toss gently, and adjust seasonings to taste.

 What are microgreens? They're small, edible greens that are primarily used to finish off a dish. They are readily available in most supermarket produce sections, but if you can't find them, baby arugula works well as a substitute.

SUMMER HOLIDAYS POTATO SALAD

For a Fourth of July party or a Labor Day picnic, what could be more perfect than this recipe with red, white, and blue potatoes? A fresh, colorful salad with a white wine vinaigrette is a modern approach to a summer favorite.

SERVES 6

1½ pounds mixed baby red-skinned, baby Yukon gold, and baby purple potatoes, halved

3 tablespoons white wine vinegar, divided

Kosher salt and black pepper

2 teaspoons Dijon mustard

½ teaspoon sugar

½ cup olive oil

One 14-ounce can hearts of palm, well drained and sliced

½ cup jarred piquillo peppers (or any roasted red peppers), drained and sliced

DIRECTIONS

1. Put potatoes in a pan and cover with cold water. Add 1 tablespoon of the white vinegar and 1 tablespoon of kosher salt. Bring to a boil, reduce heat, and simmer until potatoes are tender, but not mushy. Drain well and cool.

2. For the dressing, whisk together the remaining vinegar, the Dijon mustard, the sugar, and ½ teaspoon each salt and black pepper. Drizzle in the olive oil, whisking until well blended.

3. To serve, place cooked potatoes in a shallow bowl and top with hearts of palm and the piquillo peppers. Drizzle dressing over all.

 TIP Piquillo peppers, which originate in Spain, have a sweet taste with no heat. They're commonly found in jars in supermarkets or international markets. The sweetness of these peppers works especially well in this dish, along with the hearts of palm, which add some tartness.

GRILLED VEGGIE & POTATO SALAD SKEWERS

with Parsley Gremolata

These skewers are the perfect dish for a cookout or a summer potluck. The prep work is simple, and the result is delicious. Plus, I guarantee it will be the fanciest potato salad at the party.

SERVES 6

For the Parsley Gremolata:

1 large bunch of flat-leaf parsley

Zest and juice of 1 lemon

2 crushed garlic cloves

2 tablespoon olive oil

Salt and freshly ground black pepper

For the Skewers:

24 baby potatoes, mixed varieties

2 zucchini, sliced into 1-inch half-moons

1 yellow bell pepper, cut into 1-inch pieces

1 red onion, cut into 1-inch chunks

24 grape or small cherry tomatoes

¼ cup mayonnaise

Salt and freshly ground black pepper

12 long wooden skewers

DIRECTIONS

1. Place parsley, lemon zest and lemon juice, garlic, olive oil, salt, and black pepper in a food processor and pulse until mixture is roughly chopped (similar to pesto). Put gremolata in a small serving bowl and cover it until ready to use, up to 4 hours.

2. Make the skewers: Boil potatoes in salted water until cooked, but still firm.

3. Alternately thread potatoes, zucchini, bell pepper, red onion, and tomatoes onto skewers.

4. Brush skewered vegetables with mayo and season with salt and pepper.

5. Grill until slightly charred, about 6–8 minutes each side. Serve skewers with the Parsley Gremolata.

 Gremolata is an Italian condiment traditionally made from parsley, lemon, and garlic. It's often served with meats, but it complements these grilled vegetables very well.

NIÇOISE POTATO SALAD

with Lemon-Shallot Dressing

This is our interpretation of the wonderful French classic, the Niçoise salad. Traditionally from Provence, this composed salad is rich in protein, lovely to look at, and even lovelier to eat. Key ingredients are Niçoise olives and oil-packed tuna. For a picnic, this salad, a crusty baguette, and a chilled, dry white wine are pretty much nirvana on the plate.

SERVES 4

For the Lemon-Shallot Dressing:

⅓ cup olive oil

2 tablespoons fresh lemon juice

2 garlic cloves, minced

Kosher salt

1 tablespoon Dijon mustard

1 shallot, minced

Freshly ground black pepper

For the Potato Salad:

2 boiled eggs, quartered

1 pound fingerling potatoes, cooked and cut in half lengthwise

½ cup pitted Niçoise olives

A handful of baby green beans, steamed whole

1 pint cherry tomatoes, cut in half

½ of an English cucumber or 3 small Persian cucumbers, thinly sliced

10 radishes, thinly sliced

12 ounces good-quality, oil-packed canned tuna, drained and chunked

Freshly ground black pepper

DIRECTIONS

1. Whisk together all dressing ingredients until mixed well.

2. On a large serving platter, arrange salad ingredients in rows across the platter. Cover and chill until ready to serve.

3. When ready to serve, drizzle ingredients with dressing and finish with additional ground black pepper.

 Niçoise olives can be found in most supermarket delis. They're also easy and affordable to buy online. If you can't find them already pitted, be sure to warn your guests.

GRILLED FLANK STEAK & POTATO SALAD TOSTADOS

with Chimichurri Sauce

A riff on a classic taco you can find served all over South and Central America, as well as most of the USA these days. Instead of using soft flour or corn tortillas, this recipe starts with flat, crispy tostadas. This delicious recipe is perfect for a do-it-yourself tostado bar as well. Serve with a cold Mexican or South American beer.

SERVES 4

For the Chimichurri Sauce:

1 cup packed Italian parsley

¼ cup packed cilantro

2 tablespoon fresh oregano

2 garlic cloves, smashed

½ teaspoon red pepper flakes

½ teaspoon ground cumin

½ cup olive oil

⅓ cup red wine vinegar

Sea salt to taste

For the Tostados:

Crisp flat tostadas

Shredded Romaine lettuce

1–2 cups leftover potato salad (homemade or store-bought)

1 pound flank steak, marinated in lime juice and taco seasoning, then grilled and thinly sliced

Avocado slices

Jalapeño peppers, thinly sliced

Lime wedges

DIRECTIONS

1. Make the chimichurri sauce: put parsley, cilantro, oregano, garlic, red pepper flakes, and cumin in a food processor. Pulse a few times.

2. Add olive oil, vinegar, and a pinch of sea salt. Purée ingredients. Pour into a jar with a tight-fitting lid and let stand until ready to use. Chill if making ahead of time.

3. Assemble the salads: Spread 8 tostadas out on a flat surface or on plates. Top each tostada with lettuce, a generous spoonful of potato salad, a couple of slices of flank steak, and a drizzle of chimichurri sauce. Finish with slices of avocado, jalapeño, and lime wedges.

 TIP Chimichurri is a green sauce from Argentina that's particularly delicious on grilled meats. The basic recipe has parsley, garlic, olive oil, oregano, and vinegar: this version adds cilantro and cumin.

CHIPOTLE CORN POTATO SALAD

Cooler seasons call for bolder, more complex potato salads, such as this one with the rich flavors of chiles and sweet corn. With spicy and sweet mixed together in one bowl, it's perfect for autumn meals. And if ever a potato salad called for a glass of cold beer, this one is it!

SERVES 6

3 pounds red-skinned potatoes

½ cup olive-oil-based mayonnaise

2–4 tablespoons chopped chipotle peppers in adobo sauce

1–2 tablespoons fresh lime juice

1 ear sweet fresh corn, husks and silks removed (about ¾ cup)

Salt and black pepper

DIRECTIONS

1. Cover potatoes with cold, salted water and bring to a boil. Reduce heat and simmer until softened, but not mushy. Cool potatoes completely. Cut into 2-inch pieces.

2. Cut corn kernels off the cob.

3. In a bowl, combine mayonnaise, chipotle peppers with adobo sauce, lime juice, and corn, stirring to blend. Add potatoes and toss gently. Season to taste with salt and pepper. Add more chipotles if you like a spicier potato salad.

This potato salad can be made one day ahead. Serve chilled.

 TIP Chipotle peppers in adobo sauce are sold in small cans in most supermarkets and international groceries. Chipotles are small peppers, often jalapeños, that have been dried using a smoking process that turns them a dark color and gives them a distinct smoky flavor. In this recipe, the sweet corn, lime juice, and mayonnaise help cut the heat of the chipotles.

SOUTHWESTERN SWEET POTATO SALAD

Some recipes combine flavors, textures, and ingredients in ways that are just about perfect. This salad, made with sweet potatoes, is one of them. While each element of the salad stands out on its own, together they become something transcendent. Tender sweet potatoes, rich avocados, crunchy jicama, lime juice, and cilantro—it all elevates potato salad to an entirely new culinary level.

SERVES 6

4 medium sweet potatoes, peeled and cut into ¾-inch slices

1 tablespoon olive oil

Salt and black pepper

1 ear sweet corn, husks and silks removed

One 14-ounce can black beans, rinsed and drained

½ cup roasted red bell pepper, chopped

1 scallion, chopped

¼ cup cilantro, chopped, plus extra for garnish

1 avocado, chopped

½ small jicama, peeled and cut into sticks

Juice of 2 limes, plus extra lime wedges for serving

DIRECTIONS

1. Preheat oven to 400 degrees.

2. Toss sweet potato slices with olive oil, salt, and pepper. Lay slices in a single layer on baking sheet lined with parchment paper. Roast for about 15 minutes. Potato slices should still be firm. Let cool.

3. Cut sweet potatoes into bite-size cubes and put in large mixing bowl.

4. Cut corn kernels off the cob (uncooked) and add to the potatoes.

5. Fold in black beans, red bell pepper, scallion, cilantro, avocado, and jicama. Drizzle lime juice over salad and stir gently. Season with salt and pepper to taste.

   Serve at room temperature or chilled, with wedges of lime and additional cilantro if desired.

 Sweet potatoes are rich in calcium, iron, magnesium, phosphorus, potassium, sodium, and zinc. They're also high in complex carbohydrates, dietary fiber, and beta-carotene, so they make a great addition to your diet.

SPICY KOREAN POTATO SALAD

If you're a fan of Asian food, then this potato salad will appeal to you. Baby potatoes are tossed with kimchi and Sriracha sauce to give your taste buds a wake-up call, and it's served up on a bed of fresh bok choy.

SERVES

2 pounds small white or yellow potatoes

½ cup mayonnaise

2 tablespoons minced scallion bottoms, green tops reserved for garnish

½ cup chopped kimchi

2 tablespoons ketchup

1 tablespoon lime juice

2 tablespoons Sriracha sauce

Salt and black pepper to taste

½ cup shredded carrots

2 bunches baby bok choy, divided

DIRECTIONS

1. Bring potatoes to boil over medium-high heat in a pot of cold salted water. Cook just until tender. Drain and cool completely. If potatoes are bite size, leave them whole; otherwise, cut them into chunks.

2. For the dressing, whisk together the mayo, scallion, kimchi, ketchup, lime juice, Sriracha, salt, and pepper. Taste and adjust seasonings.

3. Place potatoes in a bowl with shredded carrots. Chop one bunch of baby bok choy and add to bowl. Gently toss with half the dressing. Cover and chill until ready to serve.

4. When ready to serve, add remaining dressing to taste, tossing gently. Serve on remaining bok choy. Garnish with sliced scallion tops if desired.

 Kimchi, a condiment made of fermented vegetables and seasonings is the national dish of Korea—and it's making its mark in American cuisine. It often contains cabbage, onions, cucumbers, and radishes and is spicy, sweet, and sour in varying degrees. There are literally hundreds of types. Look for it in the refrigerated area of your supermarket or international market.

LAYERED CORNBREAD SWEET POTATO SALAD

Cornbread salads are easy to make, but they can look pretty spectacular when the ingredients are layered in a bowl and drizzled with dressing. This recipe is best made a few hours ahead of serving time, so it's perfect at a tailgating party or as an entrée salad for dinner guests.

SERVES **6**

For the Dressing:

¾ cup olive oil mayonnaise

½ cup plain greek yogurt

1 tablespoon dried Italian herb mixture

Dash of garlic powder

¼ cup red wine vinegar

Salt and freshly ground black pepper

For the Salad:

1 package cornbread mix, cooked according to directions and cubed

½ English cucumber, sliced

1 red bell pepper, diced (¼ reserved for garnish)

1 cup frozen corn, thawed and drained

One 14-ounce can black beans, rinsed and drained

2 large sweet potatoes, peeled and cubed, cooked in hot salted water and drained

1 cup shredded white cheddar

2 scallions, thinly sliced

DIRECTIONS

1. Mix together all dressing ingredients. Whisk to blend. Taste and adjust seasonings.

2. In a glass bowl, build the salad in layers, beginning at the bottom of the bowl, using half of each ingredient: cornbread, cucumber, red bell pepper, corn, black beans, sweet potatoes, cheddar, and scallions. Drizzle half the dressing over the layers.

3. Repeat layering with remaining ingredients and top with remaining dressing.

4. Sprinkle reserved red bell pepper over the top and cover tightly. Let sit at room temperature for at least one hour before serving.

 When you cook sweet potatoes for another dish, do a few extra, chill them overnight, and use them the next day to make this salad.

LEFTOVER POTATO SALAD LATKES

Latkes are basically potato pancakes. They are made and eaten all over the world. The traditional ingredients are potatoes, flour and egg, but this simple recipe using leftover potato salad, has lots of flavor. These latkes can be topped with almost any condiment.

SERVES 6

3 cups leftover potato salad (homemade or store-bought)

1½ cups dried bread crumbs or panko

1 egg

Salt and freshly ground black pepper

Canola oil for frying

Baby greens such as spinach or a spring greens mix

⅔ cup blue cheese, crumbled

1½ cups balsamic vinegar dressing (store-bought such as Newman's or homemade)

DIRECTIONS

1. Place potato salad in a food processor and pulse just until slightly chunky. Scrape into a mixing bowl.

2. Add bread crumbs and egg and mix well. Season with salt and pepper.

3. Heat oil in a heavy skillet over medium-high heat.

4. Dollop ½-cup scoops of potato mixture into the hot oil and gently press flat with the back of a spatula. Cook both sides until golden brown and crisp. As latkes finish, remove to drain on paper towels. Cover and keep warm.

5. To serve, place a handful of greens on each of 6 salad plates. Top each pile of greens with 2 potato latkes. Sprinkle blue cheese over all. Drizzle each serving with dressing. Serve extra dressing and blue cheese crumbles on the side.

 This recipe for latkes is an inventive way to use leftover potato salad which is already seasoned.

WARM BRUSSELS SPROUT, CAULIFLOWER & PARMESAN POTATO SALAD
with Arugula-Dill Mayo Dressing

Roasting the vegetables caramelizes them slightly and amps up their flavor, which is especially delicious with this peppery arugula dressing. The fresh dill adds a bright twist to this warm fall potato salad, which would be great alongside a roasted pork loin or whole chicken.

SERVES 8

1 cup mayo

1 handful arugula leaves

1 tablespoon white balsamic vinegar

¼ cup chopped fresh dill, plus extra leaves for garnish

½ pound russet potatoes, cut into 1-inch chunks

½ pound Brussels sprouts, trimmed and halved lengthwise

½ pound cauliflower florets

2 tablespoon olive oil

Salt and freshly ground black pepper

2 minced garlic cloves

½ cup grated parmesan cheese

DIRECTIONS

1. For dressing, put mayonnaise, arugula, and vinegar in a food processor and pulse until smooth and creamy. Taste and adjust seasonings. Stir in chopped dill leaves. Set aside.

2. Preheat oven to 400 degrees. Toss potatoes, Brussels sprouts, and cauliflower in a bowl with olive oil, salt, pepper, and garlic. Spread out in a single layer on a baking sheet. Roast for 15–20 minutes until vegetables are crisp and tender.

3. Sprinkle hot vegetables with parmesan.

4. Toss hot roasted vegetables with a few tablespoons of dressing and serve warm, garnished with fresh dill. Serve extra dressing on the side.

 TIP
If you don't own a food processor, you can make this dressing by hand. Finely chop the arugula leaves, put them with the other dressing ingredients into a glass jar with a tight-fitting lid, and shake until blended. You can use this method with most of the potato salad dressings in this collection.

BLUE CHEESE BABY BEET POTATO SALAD

Tender baby golden and red beets, when mingled with wee fingerling potatoes, make an elegant but earthy combination in the potato salad world. The colors alone are stunning, but when tossed with a dressing of beet green tops, garlic, olive oil, and blue cheese, you have a delicious and impressive side dish for a grilled beef or pork tenderloin at a holiday meal.

SERVES 6

10 baby golden beets or 5 regular-size beets (any color), with tops

1½ to 2 pounds fingerling potatoes, halved lengthwise

3 tablespoons olive oil

2 garlic cloves, thinly sliced

4 ounces mild blue cheese, crumbled

Freshly ground black pepper

DIRECTIONS

1. Cut green tops from beets. Rinse greens and pat dry, then roughly chop and set aside.

2. Bring a pot of salted water to boil. Add beets, reduce heat, and simmer until just tender, about 20 minutes. Drain beets well and cool. Peel beets and thinly slice.

3. Place potatoes in another pot of cold, salted water and bring to a boil. Reduce heat and simmer until just tender, but not mushy.

4. Heat olive oil in a skillet over medium heat. Add garlic and sauté until golden brown. Add beet greens and sauté until wilted.

5. Toss beet greens, garlic, and any remaining oil with beets, potatoes, blue cheese, and pepper. Taste and adjust seasonings. Serve warm or at room temperature.

 TIP Fingerling potatoes are aptly named: they're often small, stubby, and finger-shaped. They're thought to be heirloom potatoes developed in Europe. White, yellow, and purple varieties are available at most supermarkets. They have waxy, delicate flesh with a buttery flavor.

SWEET POTATO
WITH FRESH GINGER & ORANGE

In the winter, one thing you can count on at your local supermarket is sweet potatoes—piles and piles of them. Winter is also citrus season, so what better pairing than fresh oranges and sweet potatoes? Finely chopped ginger adds a unique brightness to this recipe.

SERVES 4

2½ pounds sweet potatoes, peeled and cut into large chunks

1 tablespoon olive oil

1 teaspoon sea salt

½ teaspoon freshly ground black pepper

¼ cup freshly squeezed orange juice

2 tablespoons canola oil

1 tablespoon fresh ginger, minced

2 teaspoons Dijon mustard

DIRECTIONS

1. Preheat the oven to 425 degrees. Toss sweet potatoes with the olive oil, salt, and pepper. Roast on a baking sheet lined with parchment paper for about 30 minutes, until fork tender. Let cool 30 minutes.

2. In a large mixing bowl, whisk together orange juice, canola oil, ginger, and mustard.

3. Add the sweet potatoes to the dressing and gently toss to coat. Taste and adjust seasonings.

 When buying fresh ginger, look for pieces with thin, papery skins that aren't wrinkled. If your ginger is really fresh, you don't have to peel it for this recipe—just mince it, skin and all. If your ginger is older, with a tougher outer skin, then peel it first.

GERMAN BAKED POTATO SALAD

Served warm, this modern riff on classic German potato salads includes sour cream, white cheddar, and crispy bacon—an homage to the deliciousness of fully loaded baked potatoes. Fresh dill just adds to the magic. Cozy up and have a bowl.

SERVES 10

6 baking potatoes, preferably russets

2 tablespoons olive oil

A splash of apple cider vinegar

1 cup mayonnaise, preferably olive oil based

¾ cup sour cream

2 tablespoons whole-grain mustard

½ pound bacon, cooked crisp and chopped

1½ cups white cheddar cheese, shredded

¼ cup chopped fresh dill

Salt and black pepper

DIRECTIONS

1. Preheat oven to 400 degrees. Wash and dry potatoes. Rub the skins with olive oil. Bake potatoes until softened, about 1 hour.

2. When potatoes are slightly cooled, scrape their flesh into a mixing bowl. Sprinkle with vinegar, toss, and let rest 20 minutes.

3. In a separate bowl, mix together mayo, sour cream, and mustard. Fold mayo mixture into the potatoes.

4. Fold in bacon, cheddar, and dill. Add salt and pepper to taste.

5. Taste and adjust seasonings. Serve warm. Store any leftovers in the refrigerator. Microwave to reheat before eating.

 TIP If this potato salad dries out a bit in the refrigerator, stir in a bit more mayo and sour cream after reheating.

WINTER SQUASH POTATO SALAD

with Sage-Feta Dressing

Herbes de Provence is a mixture of seasonings that originally came from the Provence region of France. The combination usually include marjoram, savory, rosemary, thyme, oregano, and sometimes lavender. Easily found in most supermarkets, this herb mix imbues the squash and potatoes with an earthy flavor and aroma.

SERVES 6

4 cups cubed butternut or other winter squash

4 cups cubed red-skinned potatoes (or any other favorite potato)

2 tablespoons herbes de Provence (or dried Italian herbs)

⅔ cup olive oil, divided

1 bunch fresh sage leaves

½ cup crumbled feta cheese, plus extra for garnish

2 teaspoons paprika

1 garlic clove, smashed

Salt and freshly ground black pepper

DIRECTIONS

1. Preheat oven to 400 degrees.

2. In a bowl, toss together the squash and potatoes with the herbes de Provence and ⅓ cup of the olive oil. Spread out in a single layer on a large rimmed baking sheet covered with parchment paper. Roast for about 15 minutes or just until veggies are knife tender. Remove from oven and set aside. Cover loosely with foil.

3. Make dressing while veggies cook. Place remaining ⅓ cup olive oil, sage, feta, paprika, and garlic in a food processor and pulse just until well blended. Taste and add salt and pepper as needed.

4. To serve, pile warm roasted veggies on plates and add dollops of dressing. Garnish with additional feta.

 When using feta cheese in a recipe such as this one, take it easy on the salt. Feta is naturally salty, so any extra might be too much. Taste before adding!

BLACK-EYED PEA POTATO SALAD

If you're from the Southern United States you're likely familiar with hoppin' John, a dish traditionally made with black-eyed peas and rice. Our recipe uses red-skinned potatoes instead. Eating hoppin' John on New Year's Day is thought to bring good luck for the entire year.

SERVES

½ cup thinly slivered red onion

Juice of 1 lemon

1 jar of pickled okra, ¼ cup juice reserved

¼ cup mayonnaise

1 tablespoon Dijon mustard

¼ cup diced celery leaves from the tops of stalks

Salt and freshly ground black pepper

2 cups thawed or canned black-eyed peas, rinsed and drained

6 cups cooked red-skinned potatoes, cut in 1-inch chunks

1 teaspoon ground paprika for garnish

DIRECTIONS

1. Toss onion with lemon juice and set aside for 15 minutes.

2. For the salad dressing, mix together the okra juice, mayo, mustard, and celery leaves, plus salt and black pepper to taste.

3. Place black-eyed peas and potatoes in a large bowl and add onions. Toss well.

4. Drizzle mixture with dressing and toss to coat. Serve in a shallow bowl, topped with a dusting of paprika and pickled okra pods.

 Do you like onions but not the way they can overtake all the other flavors in a dish? Soaking the onion pieces in lemon juice will take away the bite, sweetening them just enough to complement the dish you're making rather than overpowering it.

CARAMELIZED ONION BREAKFAST POTATO SALAD

with Bacon, Eggs, and Spicy Pepper Topping

Is it a breakfast food or is it a potato salad? Trick question. It's a breakfast potato salad. The sour-cream-based pepper topping in this dish is addictive. It combines perfectly with bacon, eggs, and breakfast potatoes. Good luck not eating this every morning for the rest of your life!

SERVES 4

For the Spicy Pepper Topping:

½ red bell pepper, cut into thin slivers

½ jalapeño diced

½ cup sour cream

¼ cup grated parmesan cheese

Sea salt and black pepper

Dash of your favorite hot pepper sauce, (optional)

For the Potato Salad:

5 tablespoons olive oil

2 medium yellow onions, cut into slivers

4 Yukon gold potatoes, cut into round slices

Eggs, fried to order

8 slices of crispy bacon

DIRECTIONS

1. Make the topping ahead of time: Mix all topping ingredients together, cover, and chill for 1 hour. Taste and adjust seasonings. Add dash of hot sauce if desired.

2. Place onions in a skillet with 3 tablespoons olive oil and cook over medium heat until onions have turned deep golden brown, about 20–25 minutes. Remove from skillet and set aside.

3. In same skillet, cook potatoes in remaining olive oil over medium-high heat until golden brown and fork tender, about 10–12 minutes. Remove from skillet and cover to keep warm.

4. Fry eggs to your liking in another skillet.

5. To serve, divide potatoes between plates and top with caramelized onions and 2 bacon slices.

6. Add cooked eggs and dollops of spicy pepper topping. Serve immediately.

 TIP Use a good heavy-bottomed skillet for caramelizing the onions. The biggest secret to success, however, is patience! Just when you think they will never turn golden brown . . . they do. It's worth the wait.

SPRING

GREEN BEAN & FINGERLING POTATO SALAD

This potato salad recipe is a light spring dish, so a white balsamic vinegar is more suitable than the heavier dark balsamic vinegar. Also, the lighter balsamic doesn't cover up the color of the potatoes and green beans.

SERVES 6

½ pound small green beans or haricot verts, trimmed

1 pound fingerling potatoes, halved lengthwise

4 tablespoons white balsamic vinegar, divided

2 tablespoons olive oil

Coarse salt and freshly ground black pepper to taste

1 cup cherry or grape tomatoes, halved

2 tablespoons minced fresh parsley

DIRECTIONS

1. Blanch green beans in boiling water for 3–4 minutes, then plunge into ice water. Drain and place in a large mixing bowl.

2. Put potatoes in a pan, cover with cold water, and bring to a boil. Reduce heat and simmer until potatoes are just tender. Drain and return potatoes to the pan. Drizzle 2 tablespoons of the vinegar over the potatoes, toss gently, and let sit for 10 minutes.

3. For the dressing, mix together the remaining 2 tablespoons vinegar, olive oil, salt, and pepper. Drizzle dressing over beans.

4. Add the potatoes to the bowl with the green beans. Gently toss.

5. Sprinkle tomatoes and parsley over all. Taste and adjust seasoning to your liking. Serve on a platter with additional chopped parsley if desired.

  Haricots verts is French for "green beans." They're often smaller, thinner and more tender than your average green beans, which makes them perfect for this recipe. If you can't track them down, just use the smallest regular green beans you can find.

SMASHED RED POTATO SALAD

with Buttermilk Dressing

Why smash a perfectly good round new potato after it's been boiled? To create one of the easiest and most delicious recipes in this book—that's why. Boiling the potatoes softens them for smashing, then they're roasted with oil and ginger to add a nice crispness to the skins and edges. When they're tossed in the buttermilk dressing, this goes from simple to sublime.

SERVES

3 pounds baby red new potatoes

½ cup canola oil

Sea salt and black pepper

1 tablespoon minced fresh ginger

½ cup buttermilk

¼ cup mayonnaise

1 teaspoon dark brown sugar

1 tablespoon chopped fresh thyme

1 teaspoon chopped fresh oregano

2 tablespoon chopped fresh chives

DIRECTIONS

1. Preheat oven to 450 degrees. Put potatoes in a pot, cover with cold salted water, and bring to a boil. Reduce heat and simmer until tender, about 15 minutes. Drain potatoes.

2. Place potatoes on a flat surface and gently smash them one by one with the bottom of a glass or can.

3. Drizzle two rimmed baking sheets with a bit of the oil and spread to coat the bottom of the pan. Place smashed potatoes in a single layer on the pans. Drizzle potatoes with remaining oil, turning to coat both sides. Sprinkle with salt, pepper, and ginger. Roast smashed potatoes until golden brown, about 20 minutes, flipping halfway through. Remove from oven and set aside to cool.

4. For the dressing, whisk together buttermilk, mayo, brown sugar, thyme, oregano, and chives, along with salt and pepper. Taste and adjust seasonings. Serve in a bowl or platter and drizzle with the dressing. Sprinkle with chives.

 Baby new potatoes are usually about 1 to 1½ inches in diameter. They tend to have a more intense flavor than their larger counterparts, so they're especially good for roasting.

OLIVE, ARTICHOKE & FETA NEW POTATO SALAD

This recipe reminds me of a Greek salad, but with potatoes! It's so hearty that it's really a meal unto itself. Serve it at room temperature for the best flavor. Nothing else is needed except a loaf of crusty bread and maybe a nice glass of red wine.

 SERVES 6

2 pounds new potatoes, halved or quartered

Sea salt

1 cup of your favorite bottled Caesar dressing (I like Cardini's)

1 can quartered artichoke hearts, well drained

⅓ cup pitted kalamata olives, well drained

½ cup cubed or crumbled feta cheese

2 tablespoons finely chopped parsley

1 tablespoon za'atar (optional)

Black pepper to taste

DIRECTIONS

1. Cover potatoes with water in a large pot. Add salt and bring to a boil. Turn heat to simmer and cook just until tender. Drain potatoes and add to a large bowl.

2. Pour Caesar dressing over the potatoes and toss gently.

3. Add artichoke hearts, olives, and feta to the bowl. Sprinkle in parsley, za'atar (if using), and pepper. Toss well.

4. Taste and adjust seasonings. Add more dressing if you prefer. Serve at room temperature or chilled.

 Za'atar is a dried herb mixture often used in Middle Eastern cooking. Depending on the source, it can contain oregano, thyme, and marjoram, among other herbs and spices. You'll find it in the spice section of some supermarkets, at international markets, or online. It adds a wonderful nuttiness to dishes and can even be mixed with olive oil for a quick dipping sauce.

EGG, APPLE &
SMOKED TROUT POTATO SALAD
with Cider Dressing

Tossed with peppery arugula and watercress and smoky trout, this entrée potato salad is exquisite. The apple slices and cider vinegar add a fresh dimension. Served with good crusty bread and a chilled white wine, it's just what spring calls for.

SERVES 6

1 pound baby Yukon gold or honey gold potatoes

2 tart apples, thinly sliced

Juice of ½ lemon

2 egg yolks

1 tablespoon lemon juice

Salt and freshly ground black pepper

½ cup olive oil, plus more for drizzling

3 teaspoon Dijon mustard

¼ cup apple cider vinegar

1 handful watercress

1 handful baby arugula

8–10 ounces smoked trout, separated into chunks

4 hard-boiled eggs, peeled and quartered

DIRECTIONS

1. Bring potatoes to a boil in salted water. Reduce heat and simmer, about 20 minutes, until potatoes are knife tender. Drain and set aside. Once cool, cut each potato in half.

2. Toss apples with the juice of ½ lemon and set aside.

3. Make the dressing: Put the egg yolks, additional lemon juice, and a dash of salt and pepper in the bowl of a food processor. Pulse a few times to mix. With processor running, drizzle in olive oil until mixture has thickened. Add the mustard and vinegar. Pulse to blend. Taste and adjust seasonings.

4. To serve, gently toss the potatoes, apples, watercress, arugula, and trout with the dressing. Place mixture on a serving platter or individual plates. Scatter sea salt and pepper over salads. Top with egg pieces and drizzle with additional olive oil if desired.

 So many incredible apples are available today in most supermarkets. Varieties like McIntosh, Braeburn, Fuji, and Gala—all of them tart, crisp, and sweet—will complement the smoked trout in this recipe particularly well. If you've never had apples in a potato salad, you'll be amazed at the delicious combination.

PANZANELLA POTATO SALAD

This easy-to-make Tuscan bread salad is even better with potatoes in the mix. The basics of panzanella salad are bread, tomatoes, and basil. A refreshing dish that uses the freshest ingredients and is easy to prepare? What could be more delicious for a hot summer day? Add a glass of chilled, dry, white Italian wine for true perfection.

SERVES 6

1 pound red-skinned potatoes, cooked in salted water, drained, and cut in half lengthwise

1 pint cherry tomatoes, halved

Good-quality olive oil

Salt and freshly ground black pepper

Fresh thyme leaves

1 day-old crusty baguette, cubed to make 3 cups of bread

3 Persian cucumbers, thinly sliced and cut into half moons (or use an English cucumber)

Red wine vinegar

Freshly shredded Parmigiano-Reggiano cheese

Fresh basil leaves, torn

2 garlic cloves, crushed and minced

DIRECTIONS

1. Preheat oven to 400 degrees.

2. Scatter potato and tomato halves on a baking sheet. Drizzle with olive oil and season with salt and pepper. Scatter with the thyme leaves.

3. Roast 12–15 minutes, until tomatoes begin to collapse but still hold their shape. Scrape potatoes, tomatoes, and juices into a large bowl.

4. On same baking sheet, spread cubed bread in a single layer. Bake in oven, 5–8 minutes, until bread is crisp. Remove from oven to cool.

5. Add cooled bread and cucumbers to mixing bowl with potato mixture. Drizzle with the vinegar, then add a generous measure of the cheese, torn basil leaves, garlic, and a bit more olive oil. Toss well to blend ingredients. Taste and adjust seasonings.

6. Cover and let sit for at least 30 minutes before serving.

 How is Parmigiano-Reggiano special? From Italy, it's grainier than other parmesans, with cheese crystals that give it that hard-to-describe umami flavor. It's available in most supermarkets, but can be a bit more costly than its domestic counterparts. Worth it? Yes—especially in salads like this one.

SALT-COOKED FINGERLING POTATO SALAD & GARLIC-CILANTRO MOJO

The salt cooking gives the skins of the little fingerlings a wonderful crunch. When they're drizzled with the dressing, they become magical. It's a potato salad for the modern world: simple with a twist!

 SERVES 6

2 pounds fingerling potatoes

3 tablespoons sea salt

4 garlic cloves, crushed and chopped

½ green chile, like Anaheim or Poblano, seeded and chopped

1 bunch of cilantro, leaves only

1 teaspoon ground cumin

½ cup olive oil

3 tablespoon white wine vinegar

Freshly ground black pepper

DIRECTIONS

1. Place fingerling potatoes in a single layer in a heavy, flat-bottomed skillet or sauté pan.

2. Sprinkle potatoes with sea salt. Add enough water to the pan to just cover potatoes. Bring to a boil and keep boiling, stirring often, until water has evaporated completely. Test for doneness with the tip of a sharp knife. If potatoes are not done, add a bit more water and continue to boil.

3. When the water has evaporated and potatoes are tender, turn heat to low and keep cooking a bit longer, turning potatoes every so often until they're dry and their skins are a bit wrinkled and covered with a salty powder.

4. While potatoes are cooking, make the mojo dressing: Put garlic, chile, cilantro, and cumin into a food processor and process until chunky-smooth. Add olive oil while processor is running, until you have a smooth dressing. Stir in vinegar.

5. To serve, divide potatoes among plates or shallow bowls and drizzle with the mojo dressing. Pass a pepper grinder to top off.

 Mojos are cold sauces made with vinegar and oil. They originated in the Canary Islands, which are owned by Spain, but located off the western coast of Africa. A mojo can be red or green, spicy or sedate. This cilantro mojo, often served with potatoes, offsets their saltiness delightfully.

ACKNOWLEDGMENTS

I want to thank anyone who was crazy enough to give me money to make potato salad. You are the real MVPs. Without you, the world would be a slightly less silly place.

Thank you to my friends. I'd be a lonely pile of butts without you.

Thank you, Mom and Dad, for your support in literally everything I do. It's liberating to know that I can do just about any stupid thing, and you will love me and have my back. Love you both.

Thank you, Grandma! I love you!

Thank you, Alex. You're a great brother, but you live too far away. Thank you for helping me be almost as funny as you. I love you.

Thank you, Frances. I love you, and I wouldn't have made it through the potato madness without you.

Thank you to my co-conspirators: Casey, Frances, Brandon, Sam, Mike, Erica, and David. You are very funny, very crazy people, and this thing wouldn't exist without you. (Also, as I expressed above, I would be a lonely pile of butts.)

Thank you to the 16th-century Spanish explorers who took a break from committing unspeakable atrocities in the New World to introduce potato salad to Europe.

Thank you, Kickstarter! Also: you're welcome!

And, finally, thank you to J, Teresa, and Danielle. You were so fun to work with on this project. Peace, love, and potato salad.

INDEX

MORE GREAT BOOKS *from* SPRING HOUSE PRESS

The Cocktail Chronicles
ISBN: 978-1-940611-17-4
List Price: $24.95 | 200 Pages

**Secrets from the
La Varenne Kitchen**
ISBN: 978-1-940611-15-0
List Price: $17.95 | 136 Pages

**A Colander, Cake Stand, and
My Grandfather's Iron Skillet**
ISBN: 978-1-940611-36-5
List Price: $22.95 | 184 Pages

The Natural Beauty Solution
ISBN: 978-1-940611-18-1
List Price: $19.95 | 128 Pages

The Hot Chicken Cookbook
ISBN: 978-1-940611-19-8
List Price: $19.95 | 128 Pages

**Rock Art: The Gig Poster
Coloring Book**
ISBN: 978-1-940611-42-6
List Price: $12.99 | 80 Pages

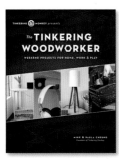

The Tinkering Woodworker
ISBN: 978-1-940611-08-2
List Price: $24.95 | 160 Pages

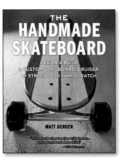

The Handmade Skateboard
ISBN: 978-1-940611-06-8
List Price: $24.95 | 160 Pages

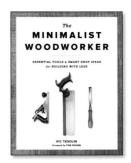

The Minimalist Woodworker
ISBN: 978-1-940611-35-8
List Price: $24.95 | 152 Pages

SPRING HOUSE PRESS

Look for these Spring House Press titles at your favorite bookstore, specialty retailer, or visit *www.springhousepress.com*.
For more information about Spring House Press, call 717-208-3739 or email us at *info@springhousepress.com*.